Sep. 2013

WITHDRAWN

TODAY'S
SUPERSTARS

Carrie
Underwood

By Mary Kate Frank

Gareth Stevens
Publishing

Please visit our web site at www.garethstevens.com.
For a free catalog describing Gareth Stevens Publishing's list of high-quality books,
call 1-800-542-2595 (USA) or 1-800-387-3178 (Canada).
Gareth Stevens Publishing's fax: 1-877-542-2596

Library of Congress Cataloging-in-Publication Data
Frank, Mary Kate.
    Carrie Underwood / by Mary Kate Frank.
        p. cm. — (Today's superstars)
    Includes bibliographical references and index.
    ISBN-10: 1-4339-2381-5   ISBN-13: 978-1-4339-2381-4 (lib. bdg.)
    ISBN-10: 1-4339-2377-7   ISBN-13: 978-1-4339-2377-7 (soft cover)
    1. Underwood, Carrie, 1983– —Juvenile literature. 2. Singers—United States—Biography
Juvenile literature. I. Title.
    ML3930.U53F73 2010
    782.421642092—dc22 [B]   2009003211

This edition first published in 2010 by
Gareth Stevens Publishing
A Weekly Reader® Company
1 Reader's Digest Road
Pleasantville, NY 10570-7000 USA

Executive Managing Editor: Lisa M. Herrington
Senior Designer: Keith Plechaty

Produced by Editorial Directions, Inc.

Art Direction and Page Production: The Design Lab

Photo credits: cover, title page Fred Prouser/Reuters/Corbis; p. 4 Jason Moore/ZUMA/Corbis; p. 6
AP Photo/Evan Agostini; p. 7 AP Photo/Josh Anderson; p. 8 Lucas Jackson/Reuters/Corbis; p. 10
Kevin Winter/AMA/Getty Images for AMA; p. 12 Yearbook Library; p. 13 Rick Diamond/WireImage
for BMI; p. 15 AP Photo; p. 16, 40 Chirs Pizzello/Reuters/Corbis; p. 18 AP Photo/Luis Martinez;
p. 19 Fox Broadcasting/Photofest; p. 20 Katy Winn/Corbis; p. 21 AP Photo/Lucy Nicholson; p. 22
Peter Foley/epa/Corbis; p. 24, 33 Bev Stofko/Shutterstock; p. 25, 41 AP Photo/The Oklahoman,
Paul Hellstern; p. 26 AP Photo/Mark J. Terrill; p. 27 AP Photo/Evan Agostini; p. 28 Steve Marcus/
Reuters/Corbis; p. 30 Mario Anzuoni/Reuters/Corbis; p. 31, 46 LTuray/iStockphoto; p. 32 Getty
Images; p. 34 Tim Mosenfelder/Corbis; p. 36 Matt Stroshane/Getty Images; p. 37, 46 Monkey
Business Images/Shutterstock; p. 38 AP Photo/Matt Sayles; p. 39 AP Photo/John D. McHugh; p. 44
Yevgeny Gultaev/Shutterstock; p. 48 Maggie McGill

Printed in the United States of America

CPSIA Compliance Information: Batch #CR011011GS: For further information contact Gareth Stevens, New York, New York at 1-800-542-2595

Contents

Words in the glossary appear in **bold** type the first time they are used in the text.

"I like potentially making a difference in SOMEBODY'S DAY OR SOMEBODY'S LIFE."
—Carrie Underwood

Carrie Underwood has become a star in just a few years' time.

Chapter 1
Dream Come True

Thousands of people packed the Grand Ole Opry House in Nashville, Tennessee, on May 10, 2008. They were there to celebrate country music star Carrie Underwood. It was a special night for Underwood. The 25-year-old *American Idol* winner was about to become the youngest member of the Grand Ole Opry. The Opry is a group of country music's most respected artists.

Country star Garth Brooks **inducted** Underwood. Her family watched proudly from the front row. Underwood tried to hold back tears. "It really means everything to me," she said of joining the Opry. "I am so blessed."

Golden Girl

Underwood won *American Idol* in 2005. Since then, her career has taken off in a big way. She has sold nearly 10 million records. Her two albums, *Some Hearts* and *Carnival Ride,* have produced several number-one country hits. The music industry has given Underwood dozens of honors. These include four **Grammy Awards**. She performs all over the world for millions of fans. Her face has appeared on countless magazine covers.

Underwood is grateful for all her success. "I love being able to perform in front of people," she told *Entertainment Weekly.* "I like potentially making a difference in somebody's day or somebody's life."

Still Just "Carrie"

With all the success, Underwood has remained grounded. She talks to her mom daily. She also visits her hometown often.

"I kind of have two lives," she has said. "There's 'Carrie Underwood,' the singer who walks the red carpets. Then there's 'Carrie,' the girl in sweats sitting at home watching TV with her dog. I'm 'Carrie' 90 percent of the time."

Fact File

Underwood was the top-selling country female touring artist of 2008.

A Grand Ole Tradition

The Grand Ole Opry began as a radio broadcast in 1925. It is the longest-running radio program in the United States. Country music legends such as Dolly Parton, Vince Gill, and Reba McEntire are members of the Opry.

In March 2008, country star Randy Travis surprised Carrie as she performed at the Opry. He invited her to become a member. Carrie pretended to think it over. Then she said yes!

◄ Underwood reacts to Randy Travis's invitation to join the Grand Ole Opry.

TRUE OR FALSE?

Underwood's favorite meal is a cheeseburger.

For answers, see page 46

The Road to Success

In 2005, Underwood was a typical college student. She enjoyed singing. But she was usually too shy to sing in public. As a teenager, she **auditioned** for a major record label. When she didn't get a record deal, she decided to study mass communications and become a news anchor.

Underwood had almost given up on having a career in music. Then she tried out for *American Idol.* She never dreamed she would win the title. "You know when they asked, 'Are you the next American Idol?' I said yes, but I didn't mean it," she told *Glamour.* "I was thinking, 'I don't know. Probably not! Don't know why I'm here!' "

◀ Underwood performs at the Country Music Awards in 2007.

Hard Work

American Idol opened many doors for Underwood. But winning the show doesn't guarantee success. Some former Idols struggle to find an audience after the show ends. Yet Underwood's popularity has grown. Her **debut** album is the biggest-selling *American Idol* record to date.

Those who know Underwood say her determination sets her apart. "She grew up in a small town. She knows what it is to work hard," music executive Joe Galante told *Billboard* magazine. "She realizes how blessed she is ... , and she continues to work very hard."

By the Numbers

4 Number of songs Underwood cowrote on *Carnival Ride*

6 Number of times Underwood changed costumes during the 2008 Country Music Awards

137 Number of live shows Underwood performed on her 2008 tour

3,481 Number of people who live in Underwood's hometown of Checotah, Oklahoma

527,000 Number of copies *Carnival Ride* sold during its first week

500,000,000 Number of votes cast during the fourth season of *American Idol*, when Underwood won

"They always tried to make me sing at everything

BUT I WAS TOO EMBARRASSED."

—Carrie Underwood

Carrie Underwood has relied on her mom for advice and support.

Chapter 2
All-American Girl

Carrie Marie Underwood was born on March 10, 1983, in Muskogee, Oklahoma. She grew up on a cattle farm in Checotah. Checotah is a tiny town in eastern Oklahoma. Her father, Stephen, worked in a paper mill. Her mother, Carole, was an elementary school teacher. Carrie has two older sisters: Shanna, who is 13 years older, and Stephanie, who is 10 years older. They are both teachers.

Young Carrie loved life on the farm. "I had a very happy childhood full of the wonderful simple things that children love to do," she remembers. "Growing up in the country, I enjoyed things like playing on dirt roads, climbing trees, catching little woodland creatures and, of course, singing."

Born to Sing

As a girl, Carrie loved singing. She was shy. But occasionally Carrie sang in church, school musicals, and talent shows. Sometimes, she won a trophy or a small amount of money. These small successes kept her going.

When Carrie was 14 years old, she auditioned for Capitol Records in Nashville, Tennessee. She tried to get a record deal. "It was a good learning experience, but nothing ever came of it," she told *Teen People*. Carrie thinks it worked out for the best. "I would've missed out on so much—high school, college," she said.

TRUE OR FALSE?

Carrie loves the 1980s band Mötley Crüe.

◀ Carrie enjoyed singing and playing the piano growing up.

Eat Your Veggies

Though she grew up on a cattle farm, Carrie is a vegetarian. That means she doesn't eat meat. She says she'd rather sing to cows than eat them. On *American Idol*, she wore a "V is for Vegetarian" T-shirt. Other stars such as Miley Cyrus, Natalie Portman, Shania Twain, and Tobey Maguire are also vegetarians. Former *American Idol* contestant Kellie Pickler gave up meat in 2008.

◀ **Carrie Underwood and Miley Cyrus are both vegetarians.**

Growing Up

Carrie worked hard at Checotah High School. She was a straight-A student. She wanted to get good grades so her parents would be proud of her. She remembers not wanting her parents to ever give her the "I'm disappointed in you" speech. In 2001, she graduated as the **salutatorian**.

Carrie enjoyed growing up in Checotah. But she admits there wasn't much to do on the weekends. Most times, she went to the movies or bowling with friends. "We were definitely the good kids," she recalls. "We'd all go to church together."

Fact File

Besides singing and playing the piano, Underwood also is a skilled guitar player.

College Life

Carrie Underwood attended college at Northeastern State University in Tahlequah, Oklahoma. She planned to become a television newscaster. By this time, she had stopped thinking about a career in music. "I had reached a point in my life where I had to be practical and prepare for my future in the real world," she says.

While at college, Underwood joined the **sorority** Sigma Sigma Sigma. Her new friends encouraged her to sing at school events. "They always tried to make me sing at everything," Underwood recalls. "But I was too embarrassed."

Going for It

In 2004, Underwood heard about tryouts for the fourth season of *American Idol*. Friends and family had often encouraged her to try out. But she didn't know if she could handle the pressure of the show.

Underwood was about to start her final year in college. She would soon graduate, get a job, and take on adult responsibilities. She realized that she might not get another chance at *Idol*. She decided to go for it.

Hometown Pride

Underwood is proud to be from Checotah. She even cowrote a song that pays tribute to her hometown. It's called "I Ain't in Checotah Anymore."

In it, she describes favorite local spots such as Eufaula Lake and the bowling alley where she spent time with her friends. "I miss the big blue skies, the Oklahoma kind," she sings.

▲ Oklahoma governor Brad Henry presents Underwood with a sign to be placed in Checotah.

Taking Flight

Underwood's mom drove her to St. Louis, Missouri, for the tryouts. Underwood waited eight hours to audition. When it was her turn, she sang the Martina McBride song "Phones Are Ringing All Over Town." She was invited back to sing for the show's judges.

Then she sang Bonnie Raitt's "I Can't Make You Love Me." The judges liked what they heard. They sent Underwood to Hollywood to compete in the show.

As a college student, Underwood competed in the Miss Northeastern State University pageant. She was runner-up in 2004.

> "Not only will you win this show, you will sell more records THAN ANY OTHER PREVIOUS *IDOL* WINNER."
>
> —Simon Cowell, *American Idol* judge

Carrie Underwood sings on the final night of competition on *American Idol* in May 2005.

Chapter 3
America's Idol

Carrie Underwood was about to step into the spotlight. *American Idol* is watched by millions of people each week. More than 100,000 people tried out for *American Idol*'s fourth season. The field was narrowed to 24 talented semifinalists. Underwood was the first country artist to be seriously considered for the *Idol* crown. And she was an early favorite of Simon Cowell's.

In fact, this tough British judge thought she was much more talented than all the other competitors. He later told *Entertainment Weekly*, "It was like everyone else that year had auditioned in black and white. She was the only one who came in full color."

The *Idol* Craze

American Idol is a spin-off of a British reality show called *Pop Idol.* The American show debuted on June 11, 2002. As of 2009, *American Idol* remained the top show on television. *Idol*'s huge ratings have led some people to call it one of the most important shows in the history of television.

◀ The original three *American Idol* judges are (left to right) Randy Jackson, Paula Abdul, and Simon Cowell.

Simon Says

Underwood made it to the top 12 on *American Idol.* Underwood took a risk during her fifth week on the show. Instead of performing a country song, she sang "Alone" by the rock band Heart.

The judges were blown away. Though there were still 10 other singers in the competition, Cowell made a bold prediction. "Not only will you win this show, you will sell more records than any other previous *Idol* winner," he told Underwood.

Fact File

Throughout her season on *Idol*, Underwood was never voted into the bottom three.

And Then There Were Two

Finally, after three months of intense competition, *Idol* had its two finalists. Underwood would battle 29-year-old Bo Bice of Helena, Alabama, for the title. His fans were known as the Bice Squad. Her nickname is Care Bear. So her fans called themselves Carrie's Care Bears.

On May 24, 2005, Underwood and Bice performed. Underwood sang "Independence Day" and "Angels Brought Me Here." Both of them sang the original song "Inside Your Heaven." That tune had been specially written to be the winning Idol's first recorded single.

TRUE OR FALSE?

Underwood has a pet cat named Care Bear.

▼ The top five contestants from season four pose for a photo. Clockwise from left: Anthony Fedorov, Scott Savol, Bo Bice, Vonzell Solomon, and Carrie Underwood.

Idol Champ

The next night, more than 30 million people tuned in to the live two-hour finale. The suspense built until host Ryan Seacrest said, "The winner of *American Idol* 2005 is … Carrie Underwood!"

When Underwood's name was announced, her eyes filled with happy tears. She thanked the audience. Then she sang "Inside Your Heaven" for the cheering crowd.

Along with the title of *American Idol*, she won a $1 million **recording contract**. She also received a shiny new Ford Mustang.

TRUE OR FALSE?

Underwood was the first *Idol* to win a Grammy Award.

▼ Underwood reacts as Ryan Seacrest announces the 2005 *American Idol* winner. Bo Bice cheers her on.

American Idols: Where Are They Now?

As of 2009, the first winner, Kelly Clarkson (right), has released four albums and won two Grammy Awards. Season three champ Fantasia Barrino starred in the Broadway musical *The Color Purple*. Jennifer Hudson placed seventh in season three. She went on to win an **Academy Award** and a Grammy Award.

Country Girl

Underwood sang all kinds of music on *Idol*. Yet she knew that she wanted to be a country artist. After the *American Idol* win, she headed to Nashville to record her first album, *Some Hearts*.

In July 2005, Underwood began her first-ever concert tour. The top 10 finalists from season four took part in the *American Idols LIVE!* tour. The singers traveled to 40 cities and finished up in September. As the tour wound down, Underwood looked forward to another **milestone** — the release of her first album.

Fact File

About 37 million votes were cast in the 2005 *American Idol* finale. According to some reports, Underwood won by only 134 votes!

Underwood enjoys touring. But her heart remains in her hometown.

Chapter 4
Top of the Charts

After her *American Idol* triumph, Carrie Underwood had a lot to prove. Some critics dismissed her as just another reality show winner. Others thought she was just another pretty face. Underwood wanted to show the world that she was a serious musician. She chose the material for her first album very carefully.

Underwood had been traveling all over the country, visiting big cities and meeting her fans. But her mind was on Oklahoma. She wanted *Some Hearts* to reflect her roots. "I just picked songs that reminded me of home and made me think 'Wow! I can relate to that,' " she recalls. "By the end, there was a theme."

Smash Hit

On November 15, 2005, Arista Records released *Some Hearts.* The album sold 315,000 copies in its first week. That made it number one on the Billboard Top Country albums chart.

Some Hearts received mixed reviews. *Entertainment Weekly* gave the record a grade of "C," saying Underwood's music was dull compared with that of other young country stars like LeAnn Rimes. But *Billboard* said Underwood sang well.

Underwood's fans didn't care what critics thought. As of early 2009, *Some Hearts* had sold more than 7 million copies in the United States alone.

Some Hearts: The Singles

Single	Billboard U.S. Charts Peak Positions
"Inside Your Heaven"	Number one on the Hot 100
"Jesus, Take the Wheel"	Number one on Hot Country songs
"Some Hearts"	Number 12 on Adult Contemporary
"Don't Forget to Remember Me"	Number two on Hot Country songs
"Before He Cheats"	Number one on Hot Country songs
"Wasted"	Number one on Hot Country songs

The Graduate

Underwood had a busy schedule. Yet she had an important promise to keep to herself. She wanted to finish her college degree. She returned to Northeastern State University and completed her schooling.

Underwood prepared to graduate *magna cum laude* in May 2006. But some of her fellow students weren't as happy as she was. They complained that people were making too big a fuss about Underwood. She worried she would be booed at the ceremony. But that didn't happen. In fact, someone asked her for her autograph as she was standing in line to receive her diploma. "We got through it," Underwood told *Teen People.* "I was just another graduate."

▲ Underwood received her college degree in 2006.

Underwood's favorite part of her appearance is her smile. "Sometimes I wonder if my orthodontist realizes how important he was," she told *InStyle* magazine.

On the Road

Degree in hand, Underwood prepared for her next challenge. In the summer of 2006, she went on tour as the opening act for Kenny Chesney. He is one of the biggest country stars in the world. He is also one of Underwood's favorite singers. She said it was a dream come true to tour with Chesney.

Later in 2006, Underwood toured with country music star Brad Paisley as well. Altogether, she played more than 150 concerts with both singers. She opened first for Chesney and then separately for Paisley on his tour. She also found time to perform some smaller shows by herself. She sang at state fairs and music festivals throughout the country.

▼ Underwood was thrilled tour with Brad Paisley.

Faith's Mistake

Country music superstar Faith Hill had some explaining to do after the 2006 Country Music Association Awards. Hill was also nominated for Female Vocalist of the Year. When Underwood won the award, cameras caught Hill screaming "What?" She looked angry. When asked about her reaction, Hill said she was only kidding. She called Underwood a "talented and deserving" winner.

◀ **Faith Hill is a country music star.**

Award Winner

In November 2006, Underwood won Female Vocalist of the Year at the Country Music Association Awards. She also won the Horizon Award. This honor was renamed the New Artist of the Year Award in 2008.

In May 2007, Underwood was named to *People* magazine's Most Beautiful list.

She wasn't done yet. In February 2007, Underwood won Grammy Awards for Best Female Country Vocal Performance for "Jesus, Take the Wheel" and for Best New Artist. In her acceptance speech, Underwood thanked her parents as well as *American Idol.* Then it was time to start work on her second album.

"This part of my life has been ABSOLUTELY CRAZY."

—Carrie Underwood

Underwood sings at the County Music Awards show in 2008.

Chapter 5
Carnival Ride

For her second album, Carrie Underwood wanted to do something new. She decided to try to write more of her own songs. In February 2007, she gathered several top songwriters together in Nashville. They were going to help her work on new material. Each morning, they broke into small groups and wrote together.

"If I got in there and wrote and it was bad, I'd be, like, 'I'm not a writer. I'll let the professionals handle this,' " Underwood told *USA Today.* "But it was something I definitely wanted to see if I could do." She proved to herself that she had a talent for songwriting. In the end, she cowrote four songs for *Carnival Ride.*

Wonderful Craziness

Underwood didn't have to look farther than her own life to find the perfect title for her second album. "This part of my life has been absolutely crazy," she explained, "and to think it all started from one little decision I made to get on that ride [*American Idol*]. That's why *Carnival Ride* works as my album title. It describes the wonderful craziness I've been through over the past couple of years."

Carnival Ride includes 13 songs and shows off Underwood's emotional range. She sings some serious songs about heartbreak and loss. But she also has plenty of fun songs. She said it was a collection of songs she would want to hear on the radio.

TRUE OR FALSE?

Underwood has appeared in a Nintendo commercial.

▼ Underwood appeared on many TV programs after her *Idol* win. Here, she is on the *Tonight Show With Jay Leno*.

A Girl's Best Friend

In her song "The More Boys I Meet," Underwood sings, "The more boys I meet, the more I love my dog!" It's true—her rat terrier Ace is the main man in her life. "He's a great stress reliever," she told *Women's Health* magazine. "He's my kid that I get to take care of and put my energy into." Ace even appears in her video for the song "All-American Girl."

▲ Underwood's dog, Ace, is a rat terrier like this one.

Back on the Ride

On October 23, 2007, *Carnival Ride* hit stores. Many people questioned whether the new album could come close to the huge sales of *Some Hearts.* Underwood wondered the same thing. "There was that fear in my head," she admitted. But she remembered that this was more about "making an album for myself that I love."

Fact File

Underwood is friends with season five *American Idol* contestant Kellie Pickler.

Underwood didn't have anything to worry about. *Carnival Ride* sold 527,000 copies in its first week. The album shot to number one on the Billboard 200 chart. That was a first for her. By December, the record had gone double **platinum**.

**TRUE OR
FALSE?**

Underwood has
performed for
U.S. troops in
Afghanistan.

Cartoon Carrie

In November 2007, Underwood made her movie debut—in voice only! She sang the song "Ever, Ever After" for the Disney movie *Enchanted.* The movie stars Amy Adams and Patrick Dempsey. It is about an animated princess named Giselle who falls down a well in her cartoon world. After her fall, Giselle finds herself living as a human being in New York City. In the music video for the song, Underwood appears as herself and also animated—just like Giselle.

On the Road Again

Underwood traveled all over the United States to promote *Carnival Ride*. Two of her favorite appearances were in New York City. First, she performed at the November 2007 lighting of the Rockefeller Center Christmas tree. Then she helped welcome 2008 when she performed on live television in Times Square on New Year's Eve. Miley Cyrus and the Jonas Brothers also performed on the show.

Fact File

Underwood's favorite splurge is antique furniture for her home.

Underwood started off 2008 in a big way. She won her third Grammy for Best Female Country Vocal Performance. She also toured with country star Keith Urban. Urban's album was called *Love, Pain & the whole crazy thing*. So Underwood and Urban named their tour *Love, Pain & the whole crazy Carnival Ride* after both of their albums.

Carnival Ride: The Singles

Single	Billboard U.S. Charts Peak Positions
"So Small"	Number one Hot Country songs
"All-American Girl"	Number one Hot Country songs
"Last Name"	Number one Hot Country songs
"Just a Dream"	Number one Hot Country songs

"Mama, it's real hard to sing when YOU'RE IN THE SECOND ROW CRYING."
—Carrie Underwood

Underwood began touring on her own in 2008.

Chapter 6

On Her Own

In addition to touring with Keith Urban, Underwood decided to try headlining her own tour for the first time. "I have been so fortunate to learn from so many other great artists while touring with them, and they have inspired me in so many ways," she said in a statement announcing her tour. "They have helped me to get to this stage of my first real headline shows, and now I finally feel ready."

Underwood set dates in dozens of cities throughout the country. And this time, Underwood had her own opening act: country singer Josh Turner. Fans snapped up the tickets. Her first week of shows in February 2008 sold out!

▲ Ryan Seacrest (far left) joins *Idol* winners to celebrate the opening of the American Idol Experience at Disney World in 2009. From left: Ruben Studdard, Kelly Clarkson, Fantasia Barrino, David Cook, Carrie Underwood, Taylor Hicks, and Jordin Sparks.

TRUE OR FALSE?

For season six of *American Idol*, Underwood performed the send-off song "Home."

Country's Big Winner

Underwood soon had more reasons to celebrate. In November 2008, she hosted the Country Music Association Awards. She took home her third straight Female Vocalist of the Year award. She also performed her hit single "Just a Dream." Her mom was in the audience, shedding tears of joy. "Mama, it's real hard to sing when you're in the second row crying," Underwood joked from the stage.

In April 2009, the Academy of Country Music named her Entertainer of the Year. She became only the seventh woman to receive that award.

Carrie's Favorites

- ✔ **Foods:** Pizza and nachos
- ✔ **Male Pop Artist:** George Michael
- ✔ **Female Pop Artist:** Kelly Clarkson
- ✔ **Bands:** Foo Fighters and Snow Patrol
- ✔ **TV Show:** *Star Trek: The Next Generation*
- ✔ **Movies:** Horror and action
- ✔ **Sports Team:** Dallas Cowboys

Giving Back

Despite her hectic life, Underwood always makes time for causes that are important to her. In 2008, she joined top female singers including Mariah Carey, Sheryl Crow, and Beyoncé to record the single "Just Stand Up." All **proceeds** from the song go toward cancer research.

In 2007 and 2008, Underwood performed for the show "*Idol* Gives Back," which raises money for poor children in the United States and around the world. As part of the 2007 show, Underwood traveled to South Africa to perform for kids in schools and orphanages. So far, "*Idol* Gives Back" has raised more than $140 million.

Fact File

In October 2008, Underwood received her own wax figure likeness at Madame Tussauds wax museum in New York City.

True Blue Country

Underwood has enjoyed success in markets other than country music. For example, her song "Before He Cheats" was a pop hit. That led some critics to say Underwood's music isn't "country enough." But she refuses to change her sound. "You can call me 'not country' until your face is blue, but I sing country music," she told *Entertainment Weekly*.

Unlike other country artists, Underwood declines to record her songs in different versions, such as rock or pop, to appeal to bigger audiences. "I hate it when country artists do that," she says. "It's like, 'All right, it's not good enough for everybody this way, so let's change it to make it good enough.' " Underwood stays true to her country roots—and her fans like her just the way she is.

◀ Underwood performs at the 2009 People's Choice Awards.

Country Crossovers

Underwood is not the only country star to have success on the pop charts. Many country stars have "crossed over" to singing pop music. Shania Twain is a successful **crossover** artist.

In 2008, pop singer Jessica Simpson released her first country album, *Do You Know*. It was the first number-one record of her career.

◀ Shania Twain is a country and pop artist.

Looking Ahead

Both of Underwood's sisters married at a young age. But she says that she's too busy to consider settling down. "That's why we're here on this earth, to meet that someone special," she says. "But I'm not looking and I don't have a deadline."

Instead, Underwood's focus is on her career. She wants to develop her songwriting and performing skills. And she says she's just getting started. "We don't know where we're going or where we're headed," she explains. "We just kind of trust and hope that whatever ride we're on in life takes us where we need to go."

Fact File

In recent years, Underwood has dated Dallas Cowboys quarterback Tony Romo and Ottawa Senators hockey player Mike Fisher.

Time Line

1983 Carrie Marie Underwood is born on March 10 in Muskogee, Oklahoma.

2001 Underwood graduates from Checotah High School.

2004 Underwood tries out for *American Idol*.

2005 Underwood wins the fourth season of *American Idol*. She goes on tour with *American Idol LIVE!* She releases her first album, *Some Hearts*, which sells 315,000 copies in its first week.

2006 Underwood graduates from Northeastern State University in Tahlequah, Oklahoma. She tours with Kenny Chesney and Brad Paisley.

....

2007 Underwood wins another Grammy Award. She releases her second album, *Carnival Ride*, which hits number one on the Billboard 200 chart.

....

2008 Underwood wins a third Grammy Award.

....

2009 Underwood earns a fourth Grammy. She is named Entertainer of the Year by the Academy of Country Music.

....

Glossary

Academy Award: an award given in various categories to members of the movie industry each year

auditioned: did a trial performance

crossover: an artist who performs in one kind of music and then "crosses over" to have success in another

debut: a first appearance

Grammy Awards: the highest honors given in the recording industry

inducted: brought in as a member

magna cum laude: a Latin phrase meaning "with great honor"

milestone: a significant event in one's life

platinum: describes an album that has sold 1 million copies in the United States

proceeds: the total amount of money brought in

recording contract: an agreement between a singer and a record company in which the singer agrees to make a record and the company agrees to sell it

salutatorian: the student ranking second highest in a graduating class

sorority: a club of women, especially in a college

To Find Out More

Books

Fisher, Doris. *Kelly Clarkson* (Today's Superstars: Entertainment). Pleasantville, NY: Gareth Stevens Publishing, 2007.

La Bella, Laura. *Carrie Underwood* (Who's Your Idol?). New York: Rosen Pub., 2008.

Stewart, Mark. *Television Moments* (The Ultimate 10: Entertainment). Pleasantville, NY: Gareth Stevens Publishing, 2009.

Web Sites

American Idol
www.americanidol.com
Visit the official *American Idol* web site for episode recaps and behind-the-scenes photos and videos.

Carrie Underwood
www.carrieunderwoodofficial.com
Check out Carrie's official web site, featuring news, videos, and tour information.

Publisher's note to educators and parents: Our editors have carefully reviewed these web sites to ensure that they are suitable for children. Many web sites change frequently, however, and we cannot guarantee that a site's future contents will continue to meet our high standards of quality and educational value. Be advised that children should be closely supervised whenever they access the Internet.

Major Awards

Academy of Country Music Awards

2006 Top New Female Vocalist of the Year; Single Record of the Year for "Jesus, Take the Wheel"

2007 Top Female Vocalist; Album of the Year for *Some Hearts*; Video of the Year for "Before He Cheats"

2008 Top Female Vocalist

2009 Entertainer of the Year

Billboard Music Awards

2005 Top-Selling Country Single for "Inside Your Heaven"; Country Single Sales Artist of the Year; Country Songs Artist of the Year

2006 Female Country Artist of the Year; Album of the Year; Country Album of the Year; New Country Artist of the Year; Female Billboard 200 Album Artist of the Year

Country Music Association Awards

2006 Female Vocalist of the Year; Horizon Award

2007 Female Vocalist of the Year; Single of the Year for "Before He Cheats"

2008 Female Vocalist of the Year

Grammy Awards

2007 Best New Artist; Best Female Country Vocal Performance for "Jesus, Take the Wheel"

2008 Best Female Country Vocal Performance for "Before He Cheats"

2009 Best Female Country Vocal Performance for "Last Name"

Source Notes

p. 5 "Carrie Underwood Inducted as Newest Member of Grand Ole Opry by Opry Member Garth Brooks." Carrie Underwood Official Web Site. www.carrieunderwoodofficial.com/news/carrie-underwood-inducted-newest-member-grand-ole-opry-opry-member-garth-brooks (accessed January 29, 2009).

p. 6 Karger, Dave. "The Confessions of Carrie Underwood." *Entertainment Weekly*, October 26, 2007, 24.

p. 7 Schneller, Johanna. "American Girl Carrie Underwood." *InStyle*, May 2008, 128.

p. 8 Dunn, Jancee. "Carrie Underwood." *Glamour*, December 2007. Glamour.com. www.glamour.com/magazine/2007/12/carrie-underwood?currentPage=1 (accessed February 10, 2009).

p. 9 Price, Deborah Evans. "Carrie Enjoys the Ride." *Billboard*, September 8, 2007, 26.

p. 11 "Biography." Carrie Underwood Official Web Site. www.carrieunderwoodofficial.com/biography (accessed January 29, 2009).

p. 12 Halperin, Shirley. "Carrie Underwood: Success Is the Best Revenge." *Teen People*, September 2006, 84.

p. 13 Halperin, 84.

p. 13 Baer, Deborah. "Carrie Underwood: The Only Bad About This Good Girl Is Her Luck With Guys!" *CosmoGirl!* November 2005, 134.

p. 14 "Biography." Carrie Underwood Official Web Site.

p. 14 "Biography." Carrie Underwood Official Web Site.

p. 17 Karger, 24.

p. 18 Karger, 24.

p. 20 "Carrie Underwood: Biography." People.com. www.people.com/people/carrie_underwood/biography (accessed January 29, 2009).

p. 23 "Biography." Carrie Underwood Official Web Site.

p. 25 Schneller, 128.

p. 25 Halperin, 85.

p. 27 "Carrie Underwood: Biography." People.com.

p. 29 Mansfield, Brian. "Carrie: Capturing the World of Country." *USA Today*, October 19, 2007, Life section, 01E.

p. 30 "Biography." Carrie Underwood Official Web Site.

p. 31 Price, 26.

p. 35 Kilgore, Kym. "Carrie Underwood Mounts First Headlining Tour." Livedaily.com. livedaily.ticketmaster.com/news/13453.html (accessed January 29, 2009).

p. 36 "Carrie Underwood: Biography." People.com.

p. 38 Karger, 25.

p. 38 Schneider, Karen S., and Eileen Finan. "Carrie Tells All! (Country Special)" *People*, March 12, 2008, 44.

p. 39 Schneider, 44.

p. 39 Price, 26.

True or False Answers

Page 8   False. Underwood's favorite meal is pizza.

Page 12   True.

Page 14   True.

Page 19   False. Underwood has a dog named Ace.

Page 20   False. But she was the first American Idol to win a Grammy for Best New Artist.

Page 24   True.

Page 26   False. Her date was Anthony Fedorov.

Page 30   True.

Page 32   False. In 2006 she performed for U.S. troops in Iraq.

Page 36   False. That was Chris Daughtry. She sang the season eight song "Home Sweet Home."

Page 38   True.

Underwood's favorite meal is pizza.

Underwood has a dog like this rat terrier.

Index

About the Author

Mary Kate Frank is a writer and editor. Her work has appeared in newspapers and magazines—including the *New York Times*, the *Star-Ledger* of Newark, NJ, *Health*, *Teen Newsweek*, and *Quick & Simple*—as well as in the anthology *Twentysomething Essays by Twentysomething Writers* (Random House, 2006). She holds a master's degree in journalism from New York University and lives in New York City.